AF271154

THE

8 ESSENTIALS FOR

CATALYST

BECOMING A CHANGE MAKER

LEADER

PARTICIPANT'S GUIDE

BRAD LOMENICK

THOMAS NELSON
Since 1798

NASHVILLE DALLAS MEXICO CITY RIO DE JANEIRO

Published in Nashville, Tennessee, by Thomas Nelson. Thomas Nelson is a registered trademark of Thomas Nelson, Inc.

Thomas Nelson, Inc. titles may be purchased in bulk for educational, business, fund-raising, or sales promotional use. For information, please e-mail SpecialMarkets@ ThomasNelson.com.

Published in association with Christopher Ferebee, attorney and literary agent, www.christopherferebee.com.

Page layout: Crosslin Creative
Images: VectorStock

ISBN: 978-1-4185-5083-7

Printed in the United States of America

13 14 15 16 17 18 RRD 6 5 4 3 2 1

CONTENTS

Welcome to the Journey 5

How to Use This Resource 7

ESSENTIAL ONE | Called: Finding Your Uniqueness 9

ESSENTIAL TWO | Authentic: Unleashing the Real You 19

ESSENTIAL THREE | Passionate: Living in Pursuit of God 31

ESSENTIAL FOUR | Capable: Making Excellence a Nonnegotiable .. 43

ESSENTIAL FIVE | Courageous: Preparing to Jump 55

ESSENTIAL SIX | Principled: Anchored in Your Convictions 67

ESSENTIAL SEVEN | Hopeful: Building Toward a Better Tomorrow . 79

ESSENTIAL EIGHT | Collaborative: Drawing Power from Partners . 91

APPENDIX | "Today's Christian Leaders" Study, in Partnership
with Barna Research Group 103

Notes 117

About the Author 119

WELCOME TO THE JOURNEY

Dear Leader,

Abraham Lincoln once said, "Whatever you are, be a good one." The sixteenth president of the United States knew that living out one's calling is a matter of stewardship. He understood that however you've been called to lead, you must learn to do it well. *The Catalyst Leader* participant's guide and DVD curriculum has been designed to assist you in this journey by helping you apply all eight essentials for becoming a change maker:

1. Called: Finding Your Uniqueness

2. Authentic: Unleashing the Real You

3. Passionate: Living in Pursuit of God

4. Capable: Making Excellence a Nonnegotiable

5. Courageous: Preparing to Jump

6. Principled: Anchored in Your Convictions

7. Hopeful: Building Toward a Better Tomorrow

8. Collaborative: Drawing Power from Partners

Leadership is not a destination, but rather a lifelong voyage. If you've been on this expedition for any length of time, you know that it is fraught with ditches and difficulties. Some days will bring great victories, record sales, and stories of life change. Others will drag you into crushing defeats, financial strain, and feelings of insignificance. You will be forced to face the good days as well as the bad—they are two sides of the same coin—and the level of your leadership will determine how well you weather them. If you are reading this and engaging in this study, you are not just the future of leadership; you are the present. You are a leader of today. And being a Catalyst Leader gives you the edge, perspective, and tools to becoming a change maker.

As you travel the road that has been designed for you, you must be intentional about growing, maturing, and evolving. The leader you will become is being determined by the investments you're making right now. That's why I determined early on in this project's life to produce an accompanying curriculum. I wanted to help leaders dive deeper into the practical aspects of the essentials of the Catalyst Leader. The eight characteristics do not work well as trophies or artwork. If placed on your mantel or hung on your wall, they will not benefit you. They must be put into practice.

This study was designed for use in groups or teams so that you'll be exposed to a plurality of perspectives. You'll encounter questions for personal reflection and group discussion. Make sure to engage with others as you walk along. In each week's lesson, you'll also find suggestions for incorporating the eight essentials into your professional, personal, and spiritual life. Leadership growth occurs in the laboratory, not just the classroom, so I challenge you to take seriously these suggestions.

Lincoln was right: leadership is stewardship. My prayer for you is that you'll learn to better steward the passions that drive you and the gifts God has buried inside of you. The One who called you doesn't simply intend for you to lead; He wants you to lead well. If that's your desire as well, then let's get started.

On the journey,

Brad Lomenick

Lead Visionary and President, Catalyst

HOW TO USE THIS RESOURCE

The Catalyst Leader participant's guide and DVD curriculum was created to help influencers put into practice the eight essentials for becoming a change maker. In the pages that follow, you'll find introductions to each leadership characteristic coupled with thought-provoking discussion questions to make learning easier. Each lesson in this eight-week study contains five sections. The first four should be completed with your team; the last one is for individual reflection.

STUDY: A brief introduction to the leadership essential examined in this lesson. General questions are provided to encourage participants to begin thinking more deeply about the trait. Questions can be answered corporately with a facilitator or in small groups.

WATCH: A short paragraph introducing the week's film clip from the DVD curriculum. After reading this aloud, play the film clip for the entire group.

INTERACT: A series of questions intended for the purpose of brainstorming a list of direct ways to apply this trait to the participants' environment.

APPLY: Specific and practical tips for making the essential part of the normal routine in all areas of participants' lives: personal, spiritual, and organizational.

REFLECT: Space to journal between lessons about what the participant has learned concerning this trait, how he or she has decided to change or adjust as a result, and successes seen as a result.

Finally, keep in mind that this guide is intended to be a complement to, not a replacement for, *The Catalyst Leader: 8 Essentials for Becoming a Change Maker*. The ideas you will encounter in the pages that follow are not complete and are best understood in context of the book itself. The participant's guide will often reference the book, so keep it nearby as you work through this study.

CALLED

FINDING YOUR UNIQUENESS

 *STUDY*

The calling God has placed on your life is one of the most important discoveries you'll ever make. Many people wander aimlessly through life with no sense of purpose. They accept job offers, move across the continent, or make life-altering decisions based on money, familiarity, or the possibility for advancement. But could it be that in our jockeying for "success" we may be missing out on the thing God has designed for us in this moment?

Ever since I was young I've felt a call deep down in my gut to lead. I loved being in front of people, influencing their thinking, and holding their attention. I was even willing to make a fool of myself in order to get others to laugh. In college I felt as though I needed to know everyone. When I joined a fraternity, I started a Bible study that attracted lots of leaders from different backgrounds and networks and "rival" fraternity houses (and, of course, sorority houses as well). I sensed something inside me that pushed me to gather, connect, and inspire others. I didn't know the specific vocational plans God had for me at the time, but I knew He'd marked out a path for me if I was willing to look for it.

I'm often asked if leaders are born or made. I never know how to answer this—I suspect it's often some mix of the two—but I know that key clues to our calling are often in plain sight, usually from a very young age. When I was working for *Life@Work* magazine, we defined calling as "God's personal invitation for me to work on His agenda, using the talents I've been given in ways that are eternally significant." But, practically, I've often leaned on this simple equation:

Natural Talents + Inborn Passions = Divine Calling

Where your greatest strengths and deepest passions intersect is where your sense of calling is usually found. If you believe that natural talents are a gift given by God and inborn passions have been placed inside you by the One who made you, then it follows that God has planned something special for you where those two elements intersect. Unfortunately, most people haven't traced their gifts and passions to the locus of intersection. As a result, they end up living life on whims built on circumstances or ambitions.

But finding one's calling is too significant to hang on the nailhead of a whim. After all, you only get to travel this journey called life once. You'll never relive today. Life is too short to spend it enduring or even suffering forty or more hours per week at your job. I realize that every hour of your workday can't be glamorous or exciting. Every job requires expending energy on mundane but necessary tasks. But if you dread climbing out of the bed Monday through Friday, you must make a change. We tend to make calling mysterious. Don't overcomplicate your calling and purpose. Sometimes true purpose is right in front of you. You may already be connected to it.

> "Instead of wondering what your next vacation is, maybe you should set up a life you don't need to escape from."[1]
>
> —Seth Godin, best-selling author

Be warned. This journey of discovery is not always easy. The pursuit of purpose is hard work, takes time, and often requires great sacrifice. Yet, the reward waiting at the destination exceeds the price of traveling there. As author and A21 Campaign founder Christine Caine has said, "Our sense of calling should be like an unfolding epic adventure."[2]

You have to be intentional when pursuing your calling. For most of us, it takes time and intensity and a sense of perspective. As Erwin McManus has stated, "You are pursuing the wrong dream (and calling) if you only find fulfillment when the dream is accomplished. You can know you are on the path to a God given and God designed dream if you truly love the process, if you love the gritty work, the painful experience, the part that requires blood and sweat and tears. If that part fulfills you, you're pursuing the right dream."[3]

Are you ready to begin walking the path to discovering your calling? God has a unique purpose that He desires to carry out in you. You were made for something specific and significant. Being a Catalyst Leader begins with identifying, understanding, and pursuing God's call on your life with reckless abandon.

As you consider the topic of calling, take a few moments to answer these questions on your own:

1. Think back to childhood. What were some dreams you nurtured from an early age that you abandoned later in life?

2. What type of actions has energized you since childhood? What have you been good at from an early age?

3. Do you love the work you're doing? If not, what can you imagine doing that would ignite your inborn passions and leverage your greatest strengths? Capture a few of those ideas below.

4. If you could pursue any career path—perhaps within your current organization—without taking a pay cut, what would that be? What is preventing you from pursuing this path?

5. Connect with those around you whom you trust deeply and have them affirm your calling or sense of purpose for this season of life. Write down their opinions and perspectives in the space below.

6. Read Ephesians 4:1–16. How do Paul's comments on calling inform your own?

WATCH

Take a moment to view this week's video segment where we'll hear from thought leaders Gabe Lyons, Carlos Whittaker, Jon Acuff, Rick Warren, Tullian Tchvidjian, Bianca Olthoff, Dave Gibbons, Kirk Franklin, Michael Hyatt, Katie Davis, Brenda Salter McNeil, Lori Wilhite, Bob Goff, and Christine Caine. They'll be answering questions about how to identify your calling and locate the courage to pursue it if you aren't already doing so. Make sure to record helpful quotes and your thoughts in the Reflect section at the end of this lesson.

INTERACT

While this week's video segment is still fresh on your mind, take a moment to discuss the following questions with a small group of your peers or coworkers.

1. Rick Warren tells us that one of the things that makes him most excited about the Catalyst generation is our growing fervor for the Great Commission. How do you feel you have been personally called to participate in the Great Commission?

2. Tied to Jon Acuff's story, is there something you should quit today in order to focus more on the specific calling God has placed on your life for this season? Where are you in the waterfall? Don't compare your beginning to someone else's ending.

3. Katie Davis gives us an incredible example of how more often than not we discover our calling by stepping out and taking risks. What risk is God asking you to faithfully step into right now that could reveal your specific calling?

4. Many times our calling is determined by what is placed in front of us. Who or what should you be responding to right now around you that requires your immediate attention?

5. Christine Caine's story of calling is a great example of God calling us to a specific assignment for a season of time. What other examples of your friends, your family, or other people in your circle demonstrate this principle of responding to what is in front of you?

6. Discipline is crucial in pursuing your calling. Kirk Franklin mentions doing something you love. What is the one thing you would do even if you weren't getting paid?

 **APPLY**———

This week, try applying this essential in each aspect of your life. Here are some suggestions to get you started:

PERSONAL: Take time to draft a purpose statement for your life. Make sure it is concise—no more than one or two sentences—and clear.

Write down the one thing you would like to be doing at this point in your life. You may have to blow up your financial standards in order to pursue this.

SPIRITUAL: Make your one and only request of God in your prayer time this week to be that He gives you a clear calling. Ask Him to help you identify your natural talents and inborn passions. Express your submission to whatever He desires for your life, and request divine courage to pursue His will.

ORGANIZATIONAL: Ask a trusted coworker to give you a "confidential calling review," analyzing whether or not you are engaging your gifts and interests in your current role. If not, ask him or her to make suggestions about another possible role in the same organization you might pursue in the coming year. If no such role exists, begin thinking about where else God might lead you that is more consistent with His will for your life.

REFLECT

Over the next week, write down what you're learning about calling. As you put into practice what you're learning, record the successes and improvements you're witnessing in each area of your life.

NOTES

AUTHENTIC

UNLEASHING THE REAL YOU

STUDY———————————

Leaders will never reach their potential in life unless they know who they are and share that person with others. This sounds like a bold claim, but the longer I lead, the more I realize its truth. As author Reggie Joiner has said, "Loving people authentically is the key to influence and leadership."[1]

I'm best at being me. Authenticity wins every time. Be human. Be real. Unfortunately, the world we live in makes this essential difficult to develop. Society inundates us with images of airbrushed faces, carefully crafted public personas, and embellished stories of overnight success. Life's bar seems to be set impossibly high and pressures leaders to pretend to be better, smarter, and cooler than they really are.

If you've been a leader for very long, you've likely experienced similar insecurities. Almost every leader I know fights this battle, struggling with being good enough or smart enough or relevant enough. Ambitions beckon us to be the person we think everyone else wants us to be. That person is usually different than who we are deep down. If we don't learn to be content with who God has made us and called us to be, then we will never reach our potential as influencers. The best leader you can be in the moment is the one you already are.

> "You are in a dangerous place when your public reputation exceeds your personal substance."[2]

—J. R. Vassar, pastor of Apostles Church

I see this strong pull to be someone we're not with everyone from speakers to college students, from organizational CEOs to pastors. As pastor Judah Smith has said, "Be strong in the grace. Your grace, your gift, your ability, who God's called you to be, just be yourself. . . . Don't be anybody else, don't compare yourself, just be you. If 'You' is not everybody's cup of tea then don't worry about it."[3]

Judah echoes the sentiment of Matthew 6:33, which says, "Seek first his kingdom and his righteousness, and all these things will be given to you as well." When we prioritize God's kingdom in our lives and cast aside our selfish desires, our innermost desires are paradoxically met. We find acceptance and love and contentment—everything we were searching for to begin with.

Of course, this is more difficult than it sounds. I know because I struggle with this essential more than any other. Like you, my ambitions often get in the way, leading me to pretend to be someone I'm not. I'm often tempted to create a new and improved Brad Lomenick who has it all together rather than being the imperfect and deeply flawed person I really am. Like you, I wrestle with being comfortable in my skin—the skin God made for me.

Our networks and friends are often more perceptive than we give them credit for. In a world of created personalities, they can spot a fake a mile away. Others recognize when we're putting on airs, and they've come to value those leaders who are brave enough to bear their true selves to the world. Those you lead will more readily follow you when you embrace your flaws, admit that you don't always know the answer, and accept responsibility for failures.

Authenticity is the currency being "traded" today of how influence is created and gained. Pastor and author Mark Batterson describes authenticity as the new authority regarding your leadership. You must be willing to share both your successes and your failures, which is crucial to letting people in and allowing you to lead well. People connect with us way more when we share our failures instead of only sharing our successes.

Take some risks to be authentic. It's okay for those around you to see your weaknesses. We don't have to be perfect, but we'd better be authentic. This means creating a community where you feel free to talk openly about your struggles.

"There's beauty in imperfection. When something becomes too polished, it loses its soul. Authenticity trumps professionalism!"[4]
—Christine Caine, founder of the A21 Campaign

Becoming an authentic leader is at least a two-step process: embracing your true self and sharing that person with others. Too many leaders don't know who they are because they hide behind their influence, power, title, or position. They don't allow others to speak honestly with them. I suggest gathering a few trusted friends and advisors and giving them permission to point out where you've constructed walls. You should be warned, though, that this is a painful process.

Second, you must have a system of accountability that will encourage you to share your true self with others. These individuals must have permission to call you out without retribution when you're creating facades or avoiding blame. The knowledge you've established with this network will help you think twice before you develop unhealthy habits. Allow those closest to you permission to tell you what you don't want to hear, to give periodic reviews, and to always have the right to speak up. As hard as these two steps may seem, they will help you unleash the real you, and in turn, release your true leadership potential.

As you consider the topic of authenticity, take a few moments to answer these questions on your own:

1. What weaknesses in your life and work make you feel the most insecure?

2. Think back over the last year. Where are you suffering from "reality deprivation syndrome," or living and leading in a state that is completely disconnected from the reality around you? How have you

pretended to project an image of someone who is better, smarter, or cooler?

2

3. Reflect on Matthew 6:33 for a moment. What are some ways you need to reprioritize your life to begin seeking the kingdom of God first?

4. What are some walls you've constructed in your own life to keep others at a distance or protect yourself from getting hurt?

5. Which trusted individuals would you place in your circle of accountability?

6. Broken people typically are more real, and ultimately can be more trustworthy. How can you share more of your story complete with all the failures and frustrations with those around you, ultimately creating greater trust?

7. Living in the digital age with social media gives you the ability to create an online "profile" that is different than who you really are. This is a dangerous reality. What steps do you need to take to rid yourself of those distractions and dangers?

 **WATCH**

Take a moment to view this week's video segment where we'll hear from thought leaders Craig Groeschel, Carlos Whittaker, Lysa TerKeurst, Reggie Joiner, Mark Batterson, Charles Jenkins, Matt Chandler, Patrick Lencioni, Eugene Cho, Lecrae, Amena Brown Owen, Vicky Beeching, Judah Smith, and Mike Erre. They'll be answering questions about how to identify and destroy barriers to authenticity in your life and how to create an authentic environment for your team. Make sure to record helpful quotes and your thoughts in the Reflect section at the end of this lesson.

 **INTERACT**

While this week's video segment is still fresh on your mind, take a moment to discuss the following questions with a small group of your peers or coworkers:

1. Judah Smith tells us we are never fully ready to lead, that we step into our leadership by first and foremost trusting in God, and that we are made into the leader we were created to be through a process. Is there currently an area in your life or leadership where you are "faking it"? How can you be more authentic by trusting God right where you are as opposed to being something you are not?

2. Vicky Beeching reminds us that being authentic is being true to our core, to who God has created us to be, instead of following every popular trend we see. What areas in your life or ministry are you forcing because of an expectation or what's cool that aren't really at the core of who God has called you to be?

3. Reggie Joiner tells us that the key to influence and the key to leadership is loving people authentically—that people will better identify with us in our moments of weakness than in our moments of success. Write down any weaknesses or failures in your life that you have hidden away in shame. Pray and ask God for the boldness to share that weakness with others and watch Him use it for your influence and His good.

4. Mark Batterson says that authenticity—letting others see your failures—is the new standard and key element of influence. In the space below, write down some of your failures, then discuss them with your team this week.

5. It's imperative that we as leaders are vulnerable and approachable. Does your team/staff feel comfortable approaching you with issues, suggestions, or criticism? How do you know?

6. Mike Erre talks about staying grounded and the issue of faithfulness. Authenticity requires us to stay centered and receive our worth from God, not others. Where are you out of balance regarding the "attention of others" giving you self-worth?

7. We are raising up a generation of leaders who have a hard time dealing with reality. Are you sensing this, and what specifically are you doing with your team to create an authentic environment?

8. Carlos Whittaker talks about the power of being real and vulnerable with those around you. Who in your life can you share anything with?

9. In speaking about emulating others who have successful ministries, Matt Chandler encourages us to emulate someone's passion for Jesus Christ as opposed to what that person's ministry may look like. Think about a person in your life who has a strong passion for God. How might you emulate his life?

 **APPLY**

This week, try applying this essential in each aspect of your life. Here are some suggestions to get you started:

👁 **PERSONAL:** Ask your spouse or a close friend to help you review your social media accounts and remove anything that has been created to project a better, more successful, or more stable version of "you." Then, ask for his or her honest advice on walls in your life that need to come down. Strategize with him or her on how you can be more authentic and then ask that person to keep you accountable.

One of the great mistakes we make as leaders is trying to be someone else. Who else are you trying to be right now? What steps can you take to be more of the real you?

◀▶ **SPIRITUAL:** Make Psalm 139:23–24 your Scripture passage for the week: "Search me, O God, and know my heart; test me and know my anxious thoughts. See if there is any offensive way in me, and lead me in the way everlasting." Write this on an index card and tape it to your bathroom mirror. Each morning, ask God for greater transparency in your relationship with Him and others.

 **ORGANIZATIONAL:** Write down two or three major organizational failures you committed over the last year. Then gather your team, admit your weaknesses in these areas, accept responsibility, and apologize if necessary.

Find a confidant, someone you can share openly and honestly with. Commit to not only finding this person but starting to meet with him or her on a monthly basis.

REFLECT

Over the next week, write down what you're learning about authenticity. As you put into practice what you're learning, record the successes and improvements you're witnessing in each area of your life.

NOTES

PASSIONATE

LIVING IN PURSUIT OF GOD

 **STUDY**

Everyone is passionate about something—regardless if you're an introvert or extrovert, a homebody or a busybody, an executive or a receptionist. What wakes you up in the morning? What keeps you awake at night? What would you move heaven and earth to participate in? What do you spend most of your time and money on? These kinds of questions help us identify our passions.

As Christians, however, our passion for God should top all the rest. As the apostle Paul wrote in 1 Corinthians 10:31, "So whether you eat or drink or whatever you do, do it all for the glory of God." The most intimidating phrase in that verse is "whatever you do." Life is filled with so many seemingly unspiritual tasks, but Paul says that the ways in which we engage them is a spiritual act on some level.

Too often, Christians compartmentalize their faith into particular actions or spaces or times. Sunday is often set aside for faith because that's the day many of us worship God corporately. The church is set aside for faith because it's seen as a "holy" place, so we try to mind our manners while there. Prayer is set aside for faith so we use more spiritual language when we talk to God. But Paul challenges this notion, urging us to see faith as integrated into all of life. Our passion for God cannot exist only on Sundays or in church. It must be present in the boardroom and the art studio and the PTA meeting from Monday until Saturday.

This means that the way you treat your family is an act of worship. The way you perform your job is an act of worship. The way you speak to the check-out clerk at a local convenience store is an act of worship. Everything, Paul said, should be seen as a spiritual act.

It is enough to make one's head spin. How can we possibly live life like that? The answer is found in one word: passion.

For believers, it all starts and ends with honoring God and seeking Him. Our passion for Jesus should define us and permeate everything we do. Our passion should reveal our soul and the essence of how we view our role in the world, either as a worshipper or one to be worshipped. You'll never be a better leader than you are a worshipper, as worship reflects the posture we have toward our Creator. Worship is such a powerful weapon in the leader's arsenal. My passion for God to receive glory must be bigger than my desire for glory. God is amazingly great. And great leaders understand that the foundation for their influence comes from a deep love of a great God.

> "Your vitality is going to not so be determined by how you manage your time or what programs you implement but really your vitality and strength in leadership comes from your knowledge of Jesus Christ and how well you see him and what you actually believe about him."[1]

—Matt Chandler, pastor of The Village

The things we're passionate about leak out onto every other area of our lives. Without having to think about it, we talk about our favorite sports teams or keep our schedules open to spend time with our children. When we're passionate about something, we act differently. Louie Giglio, founder of the Passion movement, says the church should be similar to a football game with a hundred thousand screaming fans: "People show up with nothing to gain, but want to be part of something bigger and give praise collectively to a team on the field. They scream, cheer, shout, and jump to help collectively raise the noise level. How much more should we do the same to bring praise to our King. King Jesus, who deserves a bigger sacrifice of praise."[2]

If you're not passionate about God, you'll live life trying to glorify yourself. And who wants to live with or work for a self-centered leader? On the contrary, when you're passionate about God you'll live a life that places Him first, others second, and you in a distant third. When we prioritize our lives correctly, we become better leaders.

> "God created us for this: to live our lives in a way that makes him look more like the greatness and the beauty and the infinite worth that he really is."[3]
>
> —John Piper, pastor and author

So how do we nurture a passion for God? One way is to engage in God's Word. We can't be passionate about someone we don't know, and the best way to acquaint oneself with God is through His Word. So we must root ourselves in the Bible. Unfortunately, this generation of leaders continues to grow biblically illiterate, so it's no wonder we're often not passionate about God. We need to break this trend and dive deeply into the Scriptures as we seek to know God better.

Another way is through the spiritual disciplines. For centuries Christians have nurtured a passion for the Creator through prayer, service, Christian community, and Sabbath. Sabbath creates margin, which is the fuel for responding to the unexpected, and the option we all need for being more focused, intentional, life-giving, and relaxed. Margin allows for rest, refocus, and adjustments. In the hustle-and-bustle world we live in, such regular disciplines are rare. But when we develop spiritual habits such as these in our lives, we'll draw closer to Christ.

Our passion for God to receive glory must be bigger than our own desire for glory. We must be acutely aware of our small role in God's big, developing story. You can be a competent and charismatic person, but if you are not passionate about God, you're not a Catalyst Leader. To be this kind of change maker requires a heart that seeks God's glory in all things. As I often say, if one develops the right internal passions, he will increase his external reach.

As you consider the topic of passion for God, take a few moments to answer these questions on your own:

1. Think about what you invest most of your time, money, conversations, and energy in. Look at your checkbook and your schedule. Passion is shown by where your greatest treasures and resources are going. What are your top five passions in life right now?

2. Reflect on 1 Corinthians 10:31. In which areas of your life are you bringing glory to God? Which areas need improvement?

3. If you were to fully integrate your faith into your work, how might it look different?

4. How much time do you spend in God's Word each week? How does this compare to the amount of time you spend reading other things (magazines, Web sites, social networking updates, etc.)?

5. Are you deeply rooted in Christ? Which of the spiritual disciplines do you engage in regularly? Which do you think you should invest more time in? Start today with putting into practice two or three actions that will make you more rooted in Christ.

6. As margins decrease, our spiritual vitality tends to decrease. Take steps to build margin into your life. Where do you need to add margin in your life (time, relationships, vocation, financial) to provide room for personal spiritual growth?

WATCH

Take a moment to view this week's video segment where we'll hear from thought leaders including David Platt, Brad Lomenick, Lysa TerKeurst, Jeff Shinabarger, Britt Merrick, Lacrae, Amena Brown Owen, Priscilla Shirer, Francis Chan, John Maxwell, Rudy Rasmus, Christine Caine, Dave Gibbons, and Nicole Baker Fulgham. They'll be answering questions about how to rank your passion for God, practice the presence of God, and awaken to others' need for the gospel. Make sure to record helpful quotes and your thoughts in the Reflect section at the end of this lesson.

INTERACT

While this week's video segment is still fresh on your mind, take a moment to discuss the following questions with a small group of your peers or coworkers:

1. Francis Chan tells us that the moment we lose our connection with God we are off the vine and attempting to create fruit on our own. How can you make sure that you are practicing the presence of God?

2. David Platt points out that the power of the gospel takes off when the spread of the gospel is not left only to trained ministers or professionals but when the entire body of Christ is awakened to spreading

the gospel in their context. How are you leveraging your context for the spread of the gospel?

3. We are reminded to engage in the Scriptures and constantly seek to grow closer to Christ through God's Word. How is your current time in reading the Bible, and where can it improve?

4. How do you allow the love of God to leak out through you to your neighbors and community? In what ways are you demonstrating God's passion for His people through your love for others?

5. Passionate leaders evoke passion in their followers and teams. Give yourself a "passion" rating from 1 to 10 in terms of your current sense of passion for your vocation. Why did you give yourself that rating?

6. We all need to find the area of emphasis where our passion can come to life. There is power of passion in action. Where can you display your passion publicly and create passion in others?

 **APPLY**

This week, try applying this essential in each aspect of your life. Here are some suggestions to get you started:

PERSONAL: Set aside time each day this week—perhaps during breakfast—to read the Scriptures with your spouse and/or children and pray together. If you're single, find a friend or two to join you. Commit to five days in a row and see what God does. Put into practice a specific plan for learning God's Word on a daily and weekly basis.

SPIRITUAL: Take a Sabbath this week. For a twenty-four-hour period, set aside anything you'd consider work. Instead, spend quality time with your family, rest, read, and pray.

ORGANIZATIONAL: Take time to list the attributes of God. Next to each characteristic, write out how you could begin displaying this attribute in your workplace.

REFLECT

Over the next week, write down what you're learning about living and leading passionately. As you put into practice what you're learning, record the successes and improvements you're witnessing in each area of your life.

NOTES

CAPABLE

MAKING EXCELLENCE A NONNEGOTIABLE

 **STUDY**

In a world where social media splashes success stories in our faces, it is easy to think that leaders are made overnight. But don't be deceived. Under the surface lurks many late-night hours of bookkeeping, all-day marketing meetings, and grueling sacrifices made by those leaders on the long road to the top. The truth is, success in any area of life requires being willing to do whatever it takes to get the job done at a level of unrivaled excellence.

Are you willing to arrive early and stay late? Will you seize opportunities to learn and grow in your field? Are you unflinchingly committed to specific quality standards? Will you invest extra energy into improving a product or process even though it may be "good enough" as it already is? Are you willing to do seemingly menial tasks if that's what it takes to push your project over the finish line?

> "Be a yardstick of quality. Some people aren't used to an environment where excellence is expected."[1]
>
> —Steve Jobs, former CEO of Apple

These questions help diagnose if we're being capable leaders, which is why I look to attract team members who answer each with a resounding "yes." I often compare our team to the Navy Seals. We have a culture of action and excellence, bent toward "making things happen." We are able to complete massive projects with a small team of responsive and committed people who will work until the job is done right. Our team loves creating new ideas, but we're also focused on executing the ideas we've agreed to pursue. And through it all, we are able to make adjustments quickly—think speedboat, not aircraft carrier.

Our team has also realized that one of the keys to excellence is repetition. Any winning team learns that you have to develop a game plan and then practice, practice, practice. So we develop principles and plans that are transferrable to all of our events—regardless of location or scale—and we learn to execute consistently and efficiently. This level of precision would not be possible if we were always trying to reinvent the wheel.

> "Perfection is not attainable, but if we chase perfection we can catch excellence."[2]

—**Vince Lombardi, former championship coach of the Green Bay Packers**

Unfortunately, leaders are often tempted to trade true excellence for seemingly necessary habits. One of these is a culture of meetings. Though it may surprise you, too many meetings can hamstring an individual, team, or organization. The pressure to consider all angles of a decision can paralyze us, preventing us from executing on the decision in a timely manner. But excellence derives from execution.

Another surrogate for excellence is busyness. Leaders often take on too many projects to appear indispensible or because they want to maintain control of everything. The net result is a desk full of uncompleted tasks that often get less attention than they deserve. By learning to delegate and focusing on only a few projects at a time, we're able to increase our standards of excellence.

Once you've reduced the meetings and unnecessary busyness in your life, become a constant learner. Excellence can only be achieved through growth, so every leader must be constantly expanding his or her knowledge base and expertise. Read books, attend conferences in your field, and learn to ask questions of others. One of the best practices I've implemented into my life is writing everything down. I never show up to a meeting without either something on which to record notes or a note taker who is recording it for everyone. The habit extends beyond the office too. I'm taking notes when I'm in the car, at the airport, or sitting in my living room. I'll jot down titles of books I need to read, new ideas

I'm encountering, inspiring quotes I don't want to forget, and anything else worthy of later reflection. If you don't record your thoughts, you'll lose them.

> "Do what you do so well that they [clients and guests] will want to see it again and bring their friends."[3]
>
> —Walt Disney

People want to follow leaders who are credible. And credibility is achieved through capability. Capable leaders are competent. Competency provides credibility, and credibility leads to more influence. Your team, friends, and family need to believe that your word can be trusted, you will complete the tasks you begin, and you have the necessary knowledge and skill to lead.

Capable leaders hustle. They will do whatever it takes to get the job done. That includes a willingness to work harder than anyone else, stay late, arrive early, start new projects, learn more, make something way better, stand on the stage, do the menial tasks, create the vision, pass on credit but absorb the criticism, and push themselves lower while pushing others higher. It's about being humble and hungry, not arrogant and entitled. Hard work matters. Many times hustle trumps talent and skill. Everyone can hustle. Get it done and make it happen. Be remarkable. Looking for respect as a leader? Then deliver. Create results. Don't just have good ideas, but actually cross the finish line.

The only way to become this kind of leader is to make excellence a nonnegotiable in every area of your life.

As you consider the topic of capability, take a few moments to answer these questions on your own:

1. Are you one of the first to arrive at work in the morning? Are you one of the last to leave? What do your habits communicate to others about your commitment?

2. What quality standards have you committed to in your workplace? What about in your home? Specifically define what excellence should look like for the areas you influence, both individually as well as organizationally.

3. How many meetings do you participate in during an average week? How many work hours does this translate into? How many of those hours are actually beneficial?

4. Do you often have incomplete tasks waiting for someone on your team to run with? What systems can you put in place to become a team of "finishers" that will help you execute no matter what?

5. Figure out who the "make it happen" person on your team is. As the leader you need at least one person on your team in whom you have ultimate confidence he or she will get it done, no matter what. If that person doesn't exist currently, then write down the qualities that are missing from your team members and look to hire someone who fills all or most of those qualities.

6. What can you be the best at in the world? Find one task or project where you can strive for this title. Once identified, craft a simple plan to reach that goal.

 **WATCH**

Take a moment to view this week's video segment where we'll hear from thought leaders Erwin McManus, Lysa TerKuerst, Carlos Whittaker, John Maxwell, Charles Lee, Scott Belsky, Jeremy Cowart, Joel Houston, Dave Ramsey, Michael Hyatt, Lisa Borders, Eugene Cho, Margaret Feinberg, and Nancy Duarte. They'll be answering questions about how to build credibility through excellence as a leader and how to go the extra mile in your life and work. Make sure to record helpful quotes and your thoughts in the Reflect section at the end of this lesson.

 **INTERACT**

While this week's video segment is still fresh on your mind, take a moment to discuss the following questions with a small group of your peers or coworkers:

1. In reference to self-leadership John Maxwell says, "If I can't make it happen for me, I can't make it happen for you." Think of an area in your life and leadership where you need to grow and write down specific actions you will take in that area in the next thirty days.

2. Joel Houston tells us the story of being forced to take piano lessons as a child and sticking with them even though he hated it and now seeing how God was using that to shape his future. What might be something in your life that you need to persevere through and give your best effort because God is using this circumstance to shape your future role in the Kingdom?

3. Erwin McManus tells us that we are pursuing the wrong dream if we only find fulfillment once the dream is accomplished. If our dream is a God-given dream, McManus shares, we will find just as much fulfillment in the blood, sweat, and tears of the process. Take some time to think about your dreams. Are you enjoying the process or are you only focused on the finish line? How might this process cause you to reexamine what you are reaching for?

4. Dave Ramsey tells us that despite our microwave culture, leaders are created in a Crock-Pot®—that a life lived well in patience and perseverance is how a leader is created. Although you may not find yourself where you want to be right now in your leadership and mission,

what are some disciplined habits you can be following right now that will set the foundation for a life lived well?

5. Lisa Borders mentions the importance of doing your craft with excellence and how it builds credibility when you perform well. What are two or three things you can do with more excellence right now to help create more credibility in your industry?

6. Michael Hyatt helps us understand the power of creating a platform by walking your talk, and the importance of hustle and execution. Are your actions lining up with your words? What specific areas of your life can you work on this week to better "walk your talk," and by doing build your platform for influence?

7. Nancy Duarte reminds us of the power of being great, and how great leaders separate themselves from the rest. In what areas do you need to be great instead of just being good or average?

 **APPLY**

This week, try applying this essential in each aspect of your life. Here are some suggestions to get you started:

PERSONAL: Nurture curiosity in your life. In every personal conversation this week, make an effort to ask twice as many questions as answers you offer.

Find those who are the best in their industries and talk to them, meet with them, and learn from them. Whether competitors or partners, make an effort to learn from the best in the world.

SPIRITUAL: Learn discipline through fasting. For a twenty-four-hour period during your week, abstain from food and drink only water. When you feel or hear the grumbling hunger pains, stop to offer a prayer of thanksgiving for God's provision.

ORGANIZATIONAL: Establish a habit of note-taking. Show up to every meeting this week with a laptop, tablet, or pen and paper. Refuse to surf the Web, even during the dull moments. Instead, write down the important points being made and the follow-up questions generating in your mind.

Building capability into a team culture takes time. Create an "excellence plan" for your organization, including ways to improve daily, weekly, and monthly. Instill excellence into your culture consistently through rewarding it whenever you see it.

 **REFLECT**

Over the next week, write down what you're learning about being a capable leader. As you put into practice what you're learning, record the successes and improvements you're witnessing in each area of your life.

NOTES

COURAGEOUS

PREPARING TO JUMP

 **STUDY**

Every great leader I've met wants to be a part of something bigger than him- or herself. Great leaders seek a vision that would surprise onlookers, make a difference in the world, and leave a legacy that would far outlive them. Leaders like these often seek a big vision, but that's not the only component they need. They must also have courage. For without the wherewithal to carry out that dream, it will never become a reality. Or as I often say, a person without the courage to pursue a vision is no better off than a leader who lacks a vision. Courage calls us to confront and push, even when everything inside of us beckons us away from it.

> "Courage is not the absence of fear—it's inspiring others to move beyond it."[1]
>
> —**Nelson Mandela**

There are at least four reasons, as I see it, that we might fail to lead bravely and courageously:

Because we're afraid. Every pirate movie I've seen involves a treasure hunt, and every search for treasure involves peril. We know this instinctively, so when God hands us what seems to be a map, we naturally size up the obstacles. *How much will this journey cost me? What if I go bankrupt? What if I fail, or perhaps worse still, succeed?* These questions can stop us in our tracks and keep us from pursuing what God has for us.

Because we're uncertain. Nothing will shake a child's resolve faster than darkness, and though we usually abandon these physical fears in adolescence, we often retain a fear for the unknown. Whenever leaders make a decision, they recognize that plans may go awry and their choice may bring unforeseen consequences. To continue down our current path, one might reason, is better than stepping out into the darkness around us. So we stay put in the places we find ourselves, never probing what might have been.

> "The true follower of Christ will not ask, 'If I embrace this truth, what will it cost me?' Rather he will say, 'This is truth. God help me to walk in it, let come what may!'"[2]
>
> —A. W. Tozer, author

Because we're comfortable. To move at any pace—whether a snail's or a sprinter's—is guaranteed to be less comfortable than sitting in front of the fire in a well-worn armchair. The cushy seat requires no risky decisions and wraps us in familiarity, lulling us to sleep as we watch the flames flicker. Wherever you are right now—your routines and their familiarity—runs the risk of becoming your armchair, that place where life's ease keeps stress at bay. Moving will almost certainly rob us of our comfort, and many of us would rather stay still than sacrifice it.

Because we're wounded. Maybe there was a time when you conquered fears for sport, took risks even when the outcomes weren't guaranteed, and embraced the discomfort of entrepreneurship. But now you've tasted the bitterness of failure or betrayal and you're not so sure you have anything left to give by way of bravery. So you assume your courageous days are over, and you accept a less risky way of life.

> "Down through the centuries in times of trouble and trial God has brought courage to the hearts of those who love Him."[3]
>
> —Billy Graham, evangelist

As leaders, each of us is called by God to something bigger than ourselves. We must learn to listen to His voice as the calling births a vision, and then carry out that vision even when it's easier to ignore it. Step out of your comfort zone. Whatever your fears are, articulate them. Conquer them. Pray for courage. Making a difference many times starts with just simply making a move. We can't live and lead in a state of fear and inactivity. We must simply step out and make the decision to jump. As believers, as followers of Jesus, if we're not chasing after something so big that there's no way we could ever accomplish it without God, then we are playing it too safe. A Catalyst Leader is the one who is willing to answer a call, discern a vision, count the costs, and then take the risk anyway.

As you consider the topic of courage, take a few moments to answer these questions on your own:

1. Think back over the last six months. Did you feel God nudge you at any point but you ignored it out of fear? What can you do to make significant strides toward addressing this?

2. What action would you undertake if you knew for certain that you'd be successful? What would you pursue today if you weren't afraid to fail? Record it below. And then go do that.

3. In what ways have you grown comfortable in your life? Are these, in any way, inhibiting what you might otherwise pursue?

4. What are the failures and betrayals you've experienced that still sting when you think about them? Are you living in such a way as to protect yourself from reinjury?

5. Where can you make a jump right now in your life and leadership? What decisions do you continue to put off that need to be made right now? Write them down and agree to make those decisions this week.

6. Psalm 31:24 says, "Be strong and let your heart take courage, all you who hope in the LORD" (NASB). What does this idea of "let your heart take courage" mean to you?

 WATCH——————————

Take a moment to view this week's video segment where we'll hear from thought leaders Andy Stanley, Carlos Whittaker, Lysa TerKeurst, Gary Haugen, Dr. John Perkins, Hannah Song, Rick Warren, Nancy Ortberg, Charles Jenkins, Mark Batterson, Amena Brown Owen, Derreck Kayongo, Randall Wallace, and Britt Merrick. They'll be answering questions about how to move forward on a project in spite of resources, learning to own up to mistakes, and living bravely. Make sure to record helpful quotes and your thoughts in the Reflect section at the end of this lesson.

INTERACT——————————

While this week's video segment is still fresh on your mind, take a moment to discuss the following questions with a small group of your peers or coworkers:

1. Andy Stanley mentions that many historic moments have started with just a single act of courage. What do you need to step into right

now with a single act of courage that could ultimately create a ripple effect of change for good? Where do you need to take that one first step?

2. Andy also says that uncertainty creates a true felt need for leaders. Wherever there is uncertainty there will be a need for leaders. Where are there major pockets of uncertainty within your organization or project that you should step into today to help bring clarity and certainty?

3. What is the difference between safety and freedom in your life? A lot of us are living lives with the purpose of simply arriving at death safely, instead of living a life that is full of freedom and adventure. List 2-3 areas of your leadership and personal life where you may be playing it too safe right now.

4. Rick Warren talks about Saddleback Church being built on risky faith. How can you implement more risky faith into your ministry or organization?

5. Gary Haugen tells us that in order to be courageous we have to identify and own the underlying fear that is driving our resistance to step into risk. What deep-rooted fear might you be covering up with excuses?

6. Nancy Ortberg tells us that a foundational part of being a courageous leader is owning our mistakes, telling us that others will walk through fire for a vulnerable leader. Can you think of a recent time when you shifted blame instead of owning up to a mistake? How might that situation have turned out differently if you had owned up to your mistake?

7. In talking about faith, Derreck Kayongo tells us that faith doesn't care whether we have the necessary resources or not; faith cares whether we are willing to stand with the vision that God has birthed in us. Is there a vision God has birthed in you where you are waiting on resources yet really need to just step out on faith?

APPLY

This week, try applying this essential in each aspect of your life. Here are some suggestions to get you started:

PERSONAL: List ten actions that frighten you. Let a friend choose three of these that you must complete in the next seven days.

Set a goal that every week for the next two months you will make a courageous decision.

SPIRITUAL: Each morning, pray a courageous prayer. Ask God to force you out of your comfort zone and give you unnerving opportunities to do something bold that day. Make sure to record how God answers these prayers in the Reflect section.

ORGANIZATIONAL: Gather your team and set a nearly impossible goal together. Refuse to stop working until those goals have been met, and make a pact together that you will help each other complete their part of the task.

During a visit with Bob Goff at his home, he talked to me about "quit Thursdays." What do you need to quit on? Say no to some things on your plate and focus on one thing this year. Go after this one thing relentlessly.

 **REFLECT**——————

Over the next week, write down what you're learning about being courageous. As you put into practice what you're learning, record the successes and improvements you're witnessing in each area of your life.

NOTES

5

PRINCIPLED

ANCHORED IN YOUR CONVICTIONS

STUDY

Like the rudder of a ship, something is always guiding leaders as they move forward.

Each person must determine what that is. Will it be the stock market? One's current circumstances? Public opinion polls? Or perhaps something more objective that doesn't fluctuate over time? The leaders I know who are leading well are often guided by a set of unchanging principles.

This way of operating instills confidence in those you lead because they never have to worry about waking up one day to find you've moved the goalposts. They'll follow you because they'll come to trust you, knowing that your decisions are based on something more than a fleeting emotion or external stressor.

> "We plant sod where God wants to plant seed. He's more interested in growing our character than having us look finished."[1]
>
> —Bob Goff, author

A principled life, as I see it, is comprised of at least three essential elements. These are not the only elements but are certainly among the most important.

Humility. The influencers among the next generation who are leading well are also the humblest people I know. This creates some cognitive dissonance because they have massive and expanding platforms. In such situations, the norm is that one's head expands with one's reach. Yet somehow these leaders are able to maintain a sense of humility. They aren't entitled and don't need to receive credit for every success they contribute to. They lead without gobbling up the spotlight, and when it's cast on them, they often give the credit to God's grace and those around them.

Eugene Cho, founder of One Day's Wages, says that pride is the greatest hindrance among leaders today and one of the most frequent mistakes they make. The remedy, he says, is to "fight it, confess it, name it, and share it with others. But pursue humility without announcing it so that we don't become righteous about that and thus, have a more nuanced and sophisticated version of the same thing."[2]

Humble leaders are willing to pass on the credit but absorb the criticism, push others higher while always making themselves lower, and put the results of the team ahead of their own.

> "If Jesus rode in low on a donkey, then we should go ahead and get down off of our high horse."[3]

—**Louie Giglio, pastor and co-founder of Passion**

Discipline. This element of principled leadership is a derivative of excellence. But it is more than that. It means remaining steadfast to getting the job done and doing whatever task you must to carry it over the finish line. No job is too small, too dirty, or too insignificant for a disciplined leader. He's willing to jump in and help complete the task.

In his book *EntreLeadership*, Dave Ramsey tells a fascinating story: "I was in the truck helping unload and load [boxes]. I never thought it was a big deal, but one day a new team member wrote me a long e-mail afterward, saying he had never worked in a place where the boss was a real leader. . . . The work I did that day took me just thirty minutes, but for years now it has had an impact on my relationship with my team."[4] When a leader is disciplined in this way, his team, clients, and friends will take note.

Discipline is being faithful to the small things in life and leadership. The making of a leader takes time and, I believe, is revealed and refined through the continual steadfastness in the small things. Our character, our sense of who we are, is defined by the insignificant points in life when no one is watching, when no one really cares. The times when it doesn't seem to matter, or when it is difficult to finish the project. When we wonder, *Is this what God has actually called me to do?* When it is tempting to cut corners instead of staying committed to excellence.

This is where the foundation of faithfulness and our character as leaders is created and solidified. Jesus describes this in Luke 16:10: "He who is faithful in a very little thing is faithful also in much; and he who is unrighteous in a very little thing is unrighteous also in much" (NASB). Be faithful to the small things.

Perseverance is crucial to being a disciplined leader. The process will define you. It takes years to be shaped into the leader God has called you to be. The nitty-gritty grind of walking steadfastly in the mundane and ordinary keeps a leader growing, learning, moving, and improving.

Integrity. What kind of leader are you when no one is watching? When the lights are off and you're by yourself, when you're not on stage, when you are around the people who know you the best, who are you? These questions reveal our level of integrity and help us diagnose how principled we are as leaders. We can all stand up in front of people and look good in the spotlight, but the true test of one's character is who he or she is backstage.

Consider Peter Greer, the president of HOPE International. He continues to build this nonprofit with a focus on excellence along with growth. HOPE International is recognized as one of the leading microfinance organizations in the world. One of his secrets is a rigorous commitment to transparency and integrity, and the result is that he's become a respected leader in his field.

On a practical note, leave your ego at the door. Show up early and volunteer for the tough assignments that no one else wants. Act as though you don't belong. No one enjoys being around those who think they deserve way more credibility than they really do. Stay hungry and motivated, with an attitude and posture as one who doesn't belong in the conversation. Do the right thing without being told. Character means having integrity when no one is paying attention, no matter what. Honesty counts. Be known as the team member who is completely trustworthy.

> "Leadership functions on the basis
> of trust, and when the trust is gone,
> the leader soon will be."[5]
>
> —John Maxwell

For many leaders, the greatest threat to our influence right now is our tendency to read our own press clippings, and continually put a "wall" up around us that protects us from any kind of honest feedback.

Leaders can't be insulated. The power of accountability—both personal and institutional—is one of the great engines of longevity for leadership. Above everything else, the way you maintain integrity is through accountability. Always avoid the temptation to remove yourself from healthy accountability. Refuse the impulse to start surrounding yourself with people who are there only to protect you from reality. Too much insulation will allow reality deprivation to set in, which can be costly. We need people around us who will tell us what we don't want to hear, when we don't want to hear it.

Principles like these form the core of who we are as leaders. They will help steer us straight when the choppy waters of life threaten to veer us off course. If you want to be a true change maker, you have no choice. You must learn to anchor in your convictions. Integrity, discipline, and humility are the foundations of my character, and ultimately who I am. These character traits make me into a principled Catalyst Leader. It's the basis from which my moral authority is grounded. It can't be let go of or delegated. Ultimately, leaders are defined by their inner strengths and convictions, not the outer portrayal. Your character and inner strength determine your legacy.

As you consider the topic of being principled, take a few moments to answer these questions on your own:

1. What forms the rudder of your life's ship? What principles do you allow to guide you forward?

2. When someone gives you praise for a win created by your team, are you more likely to accept it or give the credit to others?

3. Consider Luke 16:10: "He who is faithful in a very little thing is faithful also in much; and he who is unrighteous in a very little thing is unrighteous also in much" (NASB). What little things need to get done that you could do this week?

4. Are there habits in your private life that you'd be ashamed of if they came to light for all to see? How can you begin nurturing integrity by reconciling your private and public lives?

5. To whom are you accountable? Who speaks truth into your life? Who has the right to honestly tell you when you're wrong, and make sure you stay grounded? Figure this out and put a person or group of people in place that are not just "yes" people.

6. What is distracting you right now from leading well? Whatever it is, get rid of it. Get focused on the priorities. Set up a system in which the right thing is easy to do and the wrong thing is difficult to do.

▷ WATCH

Take a moment to view this week's video segment where we'll hear from thought leaders Chuck Swindoll, Lysa TerKeurst, Jeff Shinabarger, Carlos Whittaker, David Platt, Amena Brown Owen, Jud Wilhite, Jim Daly, Christine Caine, Charles Jenkins, Mark Driscoll, Brenda Salter McNeil, Mark Batterson, and Pete Wilson. They'll be answering questions about how to die to pride, maintain integrity in relationships, and develop your personal character. Make sure to record helpful quotes and your thoughts in the Reflect section at the end of this lesson.

INTERACT

While this week's video segment is still fresh on your mind, take a moment to discuss the following questions with a small group of your peers or coworkers:

1. Chuck Swindoll sets up the power of your legacy being determined by your character. How are you creating your legacy for tomorrow by maintaining your character today?

2. Integrity matters in regard to how you do business and the way you treat your customers, vendors, and clients. Are there any conversa-

tions you need to have with a client or vendor in order to maintain integrity in those relationships?

3. Mark Batterson tells us that our potential is determined by the discipline of prayer, telling us that we should pray like it depends on God and work like it depends on us. What does the current state of your prayer life show about your dependence and your potential?

4. Mark Driscoll points us to the fact that the fear of man is a trap that every leader steps into. If we are going to be principled leaders, we must constantly remind ourselves that our identity and acceptance come solely from God. What are some disciplines you might enact in order that you may be grounded in your God-given identity as opposed to looking for approval elsewhere?

5. Pete Wilson talks about those seasons in our lives where we have a heightened sense of vulnerability and a diminished sense of power, telling us that this combination makes it extremely difficult to wait patiently on God. Are you able to relate to being in one of these seasons? How may God be trying to form you and shape you through this time of waiting?

6. Humble leaders fight against the paradox of pride. Where do you find pride creeping into your leadership? List two or three things you can do today to rid your world of pride and make sure humility is at the forefront.

APPLY

This week, try applying this essential in each aspect of your life. Here are some suggestions to get you started:

PERSONAL: Ask a trusted friend to provide accountability in your life. Describe the specific areas where you are susceptible to compromise and give him or her permission to question and challenge you in those areas.

SPIRITUAL: Humble yourself before God. Lie face down on the floor and spend an entire prayer exalting God for His greatness. Avoid asking anything of Him. Just praise Him for who He is.

ORGANIZATIONAL: Have everyone on your team do a 360-degree review of everyone else. Focus on areas where the person could improve her performance if she were more disciplined. Then challenge team members to make strides in that area.

REFLECT

Over the next week, write down what you're learning about the principled life. As you put into practice what you're learning, record the successes and improvements you're witnessing in each area of your life.

NOTES

HOPEFUL

BUILDING TOWARD A BETTER TOMORROW

 **STUDY**

Good leaders are like lighthouses overlooking a busy waterway. Many ships sail through their channels—family members, friends, coworkers, colleagues—but they are at their best when they are illuminating the way forward. This is done through regular and intentional vision casting. Unfortunately, too many leaders fail to devote time and energy to this. The ships in their waters bump into each other, run aground, or float aimlessly without direction. No one wants to sail in such a sea.

Sometimes leaders fail to develop and cast hopeful visions due to busyness. They become so bogged down with the minutiae of running their team, department, or organization, and they leave little or no time for it. Others fail due to indecision. They peer at the seemingly endless possible courses they and those they lead may chart, and they struggle to pick one. Whatever the reason, a leader who fails to build toward a better tomorrow will have a difficult time becoming a change maker.

> "Where there is no vision, there is no hope."[1]
>
> —George Washington Carver

When I'm asked by other leaders about vision casting, I always point out two truths:

It cannot be delegated. Realizing that setting an organization's vision is a massive task, leaders often desire to pass it off to another team member. Perhaps someone who is better with "systems." Or someone who is more well-spoken. But this essential cannot be delegated. They bear the responsibility for painting a picture of what tomorrow could look like and setting a course for getting their team there successfully.

I think of Nehemiah, the famous leader of Israel who returned from exile to rebuild the walls of Jerusalem. He was able to capture the hearts of the people and mobilize them in this great task. Nehemiah knew he could not shirk his responsibility as the vision caster and chief motivator of his team. He showed up ready to rally people, and some of the stones placed by his team are still in Jerusalem today.

It must yield results. Too many people develop a vision that floats in the clouds and sounds wonderful when explained, but never yields any tangible results. But a vision is not a far-off and unrealistic dream. It's an aggressive but attainable goal for what might be accomplished in the days, weeks, months, and years.

Henry Cloud says a leader's responsibility, first and foremost, is to cause a vision and mission to have tangible results in the real world. Without a real difference made in real people's lives, a vision is relegated to a pipe dream, a mission to a series of wishes posted on the wall. Great leaders demand the achievement of results that can be measured and felt by those being served.

Following Jesus teaches us a little bit about this type of hope. In Christ, we catch a glimpse of what this world could be like. And because of Christ, we can begin seeing that world break through right now. It's a beautiful picture for tomorrow, but one that yields tangible results today.

> "We have been equipped with the Holy Spirit of God, equipped with the opportunity to see hope when we're in over our heads. . . . We have a hope that the world does not understand."[2]
>
> —Priscilla Shirer, writer and speaker

Being a hopeful leader can sometimes be mistaken for hype, which can lead to cynicism. As leaders, we have to be intentional about creating environments that don't allow for cynicism. Fight against cynicism and a sense of entitlement and arrogance at all costs. Cynicism can kill a team and corporate culture really fast. If you're dealing with cynicism in your organization, stamp it out right now.

Moreover, don't be a leader who lives in hopa hopa land, a fantasy world where everything is rosy all the time and always positive no matter what the reality is. Part of leadership is to paint the picture of what reality truly is and confront the brutal facts head-on. You can't turn away or stick your head in the sand so as to avoid reality. A hopeful visionary operates on hope rather than hype. He or she knows that hype produces chatter, while hope inspires action.

People on your team expect you to be positive, upbeat, and optimistic. You have to give your team reason to believe that tomorrow will be even better than today. A Catalyst Leader is inspiring. Your energy and optimism signals your personal level of commitment to your team. I've heard both Andy Stanley and Bill Hybels mention that the best thing you can bring to your team is your energy. Bring your physical, intellectual, and emotional energy to your team. It's not about hype or pretend, but all about hope and vision. Part of your role as a leader is to lift the energy of those around you. You have to give your team reason to believe that tomorrow will be even better than today. Cory Booker, mayor of Newark, New Jersey, says he has to have "hope unhinged."[3] Constant hope. Leaders are dealers in hope and must give it away constantly and without bias.

That's why some of the most influential organizations and leaders today maintain a strong sense of vision, rooted in a better world. I believe in this current generation of leaders.

"The visionary must light a flame.
Those who choose to follow its light
must work to keep it burning."[4]

—Simon Sinek

Hopeful leaders pursue a vision that ultimately creates a personal and organizational legacy. John Maxwell says people will describe your life, and your legacy, in one sentence. What one sentence do you want people to describe you with? That is your legacy statement. Write it down.

Leaders are different than managers in that they own a vision bigger than what is in front of them and see where they want to be next, where they want to take those who follow them. Managers work on things that are right in front of them. But leaders look over the next hill. They invent the future, instead of just responding to the present. Leaders initiate.

Begin to think about what your vision might be. What's on your heart or stirring in you that you keep pushing back because it just doesn't seem possible? For us at Catalyst, we've always wanted to create an environment that fosters and ushers in hope—hope and belief that we really can make a difference and change the world.

What would you like to see accomplished as a result of your work in the next five months? How about in the next five years? Take steps toward making that vision a reality. Trust me. You and your team will be glad you did.

As you consider the topic of hopefulness, take a few moments to answer these questions on your own:

1. What is the biggest reason you fail to develop and cast vision?

2. Do you try to delegate the role of vision caster? How can you do a better job casting vision yourself?

3. Luke 12:48 says, "From everyone who has been given much, much will be demanded; and from the one who has been entrusted with much, much more will be asked." How might this inform one's view of responsibility for vision-casting?

4. When has your vision seemed amorphous or unattainable? How can you begin to shape your vision so that it yields more tangible results?

5. A leader must scale his or her vision appropriately, especially those of us who are idea creators. We think every idea we have has a global reach. Not true. What is your current vision, and has it been scaled appropriately?

6. The current state of the church around the world is one of hope and optimism. How are you engaged with the global church and Christians around the world? How do you see yourself as part of God's larger unfolding story around you?

7. One of the best ways to become an organization of hopefulness and vision for the future is to infuse your team with young visionaries. Look around your team or organization. How many of your key leaders are under the age of thirty? Assess your need for adding young visionaries to your team. Hire at least one new young leader in the next month. How specifically can your organization benefit from having additional younger leaders?

 **WATCH**

Take a moment to view this week's video segment where we'll hear from thought leaders Bob Goff, Jeff Shinabarger, Lysa TerKeurst, Christine Caine, Eugene Cho, Michael Hyatt, Brenda Salter McNeil, Donald Miller, Jon Tyson, Bill Hybels, Mark Batterson, Jena Lee Nardella,

Esther Havens, Jeremy Cowart, Brandon Hatmaker, and Scott Todd. They'll be answering questions about unifying others around a common vision, integrating hope into your neighborhood and community, and leaking Jesus into your workplace. Make sure to record helpful quotes and your thoughts in the Reflect section at the end of this lesson.

INTERACT

While this week's video segment is still fresh on your mind, take a moment to discuss the following questions with a small group of your peers or coworkers:

1. Bob Goff tells us that it's time to stop talking and start doing, and that people who love Jesus leak Jesus. How is your life leaking Jesus?

2. Donald Miller shares that the thing he is most hopeful about as he looks at the landscape of young leaders in the church is their ability to come together in unity over a common cause. Think of a personal area of passion. What are some ways that you can unify with others to create a greater good in this area?

3. Bill Hybels says that vision and creating a picture of the future that produces passion in people is the most important weapon in a leader's arsenal. Casting vision involves giving hope. Have you given your team or staff a clear picture of the future that produces passion in them? Where do you need to put vision to work in your organization to bring more hope?

4. Esther Havens spends her life using photography to tell stories of hope from those living in extreme poverty. How can a difficulty you are currently facing actually be something God is using to create a spring of hope?

5. Hopeful leaders help create hopeful organizations. And hopeful organizations help create hopeful communities. List three specific ways you can integrate hope into your neighborhood or community.

6. National Community Church has been the fulfillment of a hopeful vision that was given to Mark Batterson. How powerful is your current vision for the project, team, organization, or mission God has given you? Are people clamoring to get involved with it and be connected to it?

APPLY

This week, try applying this essential in each aspect of your life. Here are some suggestions to get you started:

👁 **PERSONAL:** Leaders are innovators. They try new things. They are willing to fail, but fail trying. Try something this week that you have a strong vision and hope for, knowing you will possibly fail.

Compose a list of the ways that your own personal work improves the world and others' lives. Post this in a visible place so that you can see it on a constant basis.

What are you dreaming about that you've been afraid to vocalize? Find someone you trust, and dream with him or her aloud today.

◖◗ **SPIRITUAL:** Make Romans 15:13 your verse for this week: "May the God of hope fill you with all joy and peace in believing, so that you will abound in hope by the power of the Holy Spirit" (NASB). Ask God to keep hope alive inside of you.

ORGANIZATIONAL: Gather your team and together compile a list of the ways in which your collective work is making a positive difference in the world and others' lives. Post the list in a public place where everyone can see it this week.

What is your message? Bill Hybels says a leader should define his or her message and vision in five distinct words. The laser focus of your message is paramount to being a hopeful visionary. What are you asking people on your team to truly commit to? What is it you really want to build, and who are you truly trying to reach? What footprint do you hope to leave? Articulate this with five key words.

 **REFLECT**

Over the next week, write down what you're learning about being a hopeful leader. As you put into practice what you're learning, record the successes and improvements you're witnessing in each area of your life.

NOTES

8

COLLABORATIVE

DRAWING POWER
FROM PARTNERS

STUDY

Years ago, I saw a commercial that rattled off the oft-repeated cliché, "We can do more together than we can apart." I had probably heard this phrase, or some version of it, a thousand times in various settings. But this time, it meant more to me. I had been leading Catalyst for a few years and had noticed the way we were growing comfortable and stale with our partnerships. I wanted our organization to be known for sharing ideas with others and interacting with, even working alongside, those some might call "competition." That was a turning point. What I once viewed as an oddity, I now realize is one of our greatest organizational strengths.

We're not the only ones taking this approach. Art House Dallas, led by Jenny White, has become a credible artistic voice and now serves as a model for launching other art houses in cities across America. Dave Morin, a former Apple employee and one of the first Facebook team members in the site's early years, took his experience and started the social networking site Path. His work is also a model for collaborative leadership.

Collaboration is on the rise among leaders today, and for good reason. They're learning that sharing increases available knowledge that anyone can access. Good ideas are released for the benefit of all. Catalyst Leaders want to work alongside others, forming partnerships from which they can birth new ideas and create new products. Simon Sinek, noted author and thought leader, has said, "Weak leaders see themselves as in front of others. Great leaders see themselves by their sides."[1]

Community is oxygen for our souls. The power of being in a tribe is intoxicating. We all want to belong. Collaboration is catching on across industries. Many of the "new economy" companies create environments where everyone is working in the same room. No corner offices, no plush closed-door environments, just open-space collaborative work space that forces everyone to work together. This is the new reality of our world. Nowadays you have to work together in order to accomplish anything. No more lone rangers. Collaboration is now a leading element to the style of leadership that gets things done in today's culture. Companies are taking notice. Open source is the new reality in technology.

"The next best thing to being wise oneself is to live in a circle of those who are."[2]

—C. S. Lewis, author

A great example of this is the way that programmers and developers are creating apps for the Android phone platform through Google. This open-source mentality is about giving away one's ideas for the better. Chris Anderson wrote about this phenomenon in his book *Free*, saying the approach is not about protecting or hoarding. It's about releasing and improving. The more you own, the more intentional you have to be about sharing it with others. In the end, everyone benefits from this kind of behavior.

If you're thinking about fostering a more collaborative spirit in your work, here are a few tips:

→ Choose wisely. Don't partner just for the sake of partnership. Make sure the chemistry, values, and vision of your coconspirators align with your own. This will save you a lot of potential headache down the road.

→ Sacrifice your pride. In a collaborative relationship, sometimes you will receive credit and sometimes your partners will. Learn to be okay with sharing the spotlight.

→ Pull your own weight but learn to share. In collaboration, you can't control everything. Even the word itself defines what the outcome should be—co-labor. Learn to take responsibility for what you can do well, and allow others to do the rest.

> "Two are better than one, because they have a good return for their work: If one falls down, his friend can help him up. But pity the man who falls and has no one to help him up! . . . Though one may be overpowered, two can defend themselves. A cord of three strands is not quickly broken."

—**King Solomon, Ecclesiastes 4:9–10, 12.**

As a leader, one of your keys to creating a collaborative culture in your organization is to empower your team. In order to grow a successful organization that outlives you, you must empower those around you. Empower your team today in a new and fresh way.

→ Assign responsibility by allowing them to own key projects from start to finish.

→ Fight for them, and stand up for them.

→ Give them more and more opportunities to make decisions, and don't second-guess them.

→ Encourage them. Feed them "ego biscuits" on a constant basis.

→ Counsel, coach, and instruct. All three of these are different from one another but equally important.

→ Overwhelm them with projects that seem out of their reach and experience.

→ Give them permission to push back, take risks, take on more, and think outside the box on doing their job better.

Both John 13 and Philippians 2 outline the essence of biblical collaboration. The world will know us by our love. The church working together and unified is an unstoppable force. This type of leadership is difficult, but the result makes the trouble worth it. A Catalyst Leader must destroy the barriers of jealousy and unnecessary competition to create a culture of celebration. If you can begin increasing collaboration in your professional and private life, you'll realize that the old cliché is true: we really can accomplish more together than apart.

As you consider the topic of collaboration, take a few moments to answer these questions on your own:

1. Think of the current realities in your organization. What is something your company could only accomplish through a strategic partnership?

2. Look around at your team's workspace. How could you make physical changes to increase internal collaboration? How can you make changes in reporting and structure in general to increase collaboration?

3. What partners might you be able to learn from if you and those around you could sacrifice your pride? How can you begin making this a reality?

4. Read Philippians 2:2–5. How might this change your thinking about this essential?

5. Bob Goff talks about collaboration and the notion of pulling your boats up next to each other to work together. What organization and leader should you be looking to "pull your boat up" next to and work with? Set up a meeting with them.

WATCH

Take a moment to view this week's video segment where we'll hear from thought leaders including Mark Driscoll, Judah Smith, Jeff Shinabarger, Lysa TerKeurst, Donald Miller, Bob Goff, Charles Jenkins, Dave Gibbons, Joshua DuBois, Claire Díaz-Ortiz, Kirk Franklin, Israel Houghton, Nancy Ortberg, Bethany Hoang, Michael Hyatt, Lisa Borders, Nancy Duarte, Kari Jobe, Scott Belsky. They'll be answering questions about building a collaborative organizational culture, how to work with those you may disagree with, and collaboration for the sake of the gospel. Make sure to record helpful quotes and your thoughts in the Reflect section at the end of this lesson.

INTERACT

While this week's video segment is still fresh on your mind, take a moment to discuss the following questions with a small group of your peers or coworkers:

1. Judah Smith shares about how the spiritual climate of the Pacific Northwest has brought churches alongside each other to work together for the kingdom in some remarkable ways. What are some ways that you might work together with other leaders in your immediate community for the cause of the gospel?

2. Joshua DuBois uses the example of service to show how people who may have different views can collaborate with both local and national government on issues that everyone believes in. What are some issues affecting your context that you might be able to collaborate with the local government on for the greater good?

3. Claire Díaz-Ortiz shows us the power that social media has in creating collaboration for good. We often use social media for our own benefit, but what are some ways you may be able to capitalize on the medium to collaborate for a cause? How could you use social media to organize a group of like-minded leaders into action?

4. It's important as leaders that we reach out to those who disagree with us and find ways to work together. How do you partner with those you completely disagree with?

5. Nancy Ortberg talks about one of the new realities of leadership—the flattening of hierarchies within organizations, which requires greater collaboration and partnership instead of top-down command and control leadership. How are you creating a collaborative culture within your organization?

6. Working together is crucial to accomplishing something bigger than what you can do alone. How well do you know the organizations with whom you are partnering? What team or organization should you reach out to today and connect on a deeper, more personal level?

 **APPLY**

This week, try applying this essential in each aspect of your life. Here are some suggestions to get you started:

👁 **PERSONAL:** Throw a dinner party. Construct the list by pairing up people who would benefit from knowing each other and then connect them after they arrive.

List out who you need help from and make the request. The best collaborators are often the most successful. Set up a meeting this week with someone you admire who is great at what he does. Learn from that person.

SPIRITUAL: Gather a group of five friends or coworkers to study the book of James together in a week's span. The book has five chapters, so assign one to each group member to share his or her thoughts. Listen and learn from the others' unique perspectives and, when your time comes, share yours with them.

ORGANIZATIONAL: Invite the employees of your biggest local competitor to your office for a lunch. Build relationships, and if possible, share best practices with each other. This simple act will force you to begin breaking down walls that keep you and your team isolated from others.

Celebrate others' success. Write a card, make a call, or send an e-mail to a "competitor" congratulating him or her on success. We don't naturally cheer others on well who might be passing us, because we think it's to our demise.

REFLECT

Over the next week, write down what you're learning about collaboration. As you put into practice what you're learning, record the successes and improvements you're witnessing in each area of your life.

NOTES

8

APPENDIX

"TODAY'S CHRISTIAN LEADERS" STUDY, IN PARTNERSHIP WITH
BARNA RESEARCH GROUP

The following survey results reflect a nationwide study of Christian adults, ages eighteen and older. It was conducted by Barna Research Group through online surveys of 1,116 self-described Christian adults in June 2012. The study probes the essentials discussed in this book. The following is a sampling of the results of this study.

I. WHAT KIND OF LEADERS ARE NEEDED?

The first question explored what Christians believe to be the most important traits that leaders need to possess given all the changes taking place in the world. Respondents were given ten different options, including short descriptions, to choose from:

1. Courage—*being willing to take risks*

2. Vision—*knowing where you are going*

3. Competence—*being good at what you do*

4. Humility—*giving credit to others*

5. Collaboration—*working well with others*

6. Passion for God—*loving God more than anything else*

7. Integrity—*doing the right thing*

8. Authenticity—*being truthful and reliable*

9. Purpose—*being made for or "called" to the job*

10. Discipline—*the ability to stay focused and get things done*

Of those ten characteristics listed, most Christians believe that integrity is the most important characteristic for leaders today (64%). On the next tier are authenticity (40%) and discipline (38%), which are followed by passion for God (31%) and competence (31%). The least important factors are purpose (5%) and humility (7%). Vision (26%), collaboration (25%), and courage (15%) are ranked in the middle of the pack.

Evangelicals are a subset of the broader Christian market, comprising 8 percent of the nation's population. They are more likely to identify the importance of passion for God and integrity, but they are less likely than other Christians to name discipline, competence, vision, or collaboration.

Older Christians are more likely than their younger peers (under 40) to list integrity, authenticity, passion for God, and courage as critical facets of leadership. Younger leaders are slightly more likely to name vision, collaboration, and humility. Still, the differences between the age groups are not great.

TABLE 1: MOST IMPORTANT LEADERSHIP TRAITS

Question: Thinking about all the changes taking place in our nation and the world, what will be the 2 or 3 most important leadership traits for people to be great leaders in the next decade? (Mark between 1 and 3 responses.)

	ALL CHRISTIANS	EVANGELICALS	AGE GROUP		SELF-DESCRIBED LEADER	
			18–39	40-plus	yes	no
integrity	64%	75%	59%	66%	65%	63%
authenticity	40	41	34	42	39	41
discipline	38	22	41	37	36	41
passion for God	31	83	26	34	33	28

	ALL CHRISTIANS	EVANGELICALS	AGE GROUP		SELF-DESCRIBED LEADER	
			18–39	40-plus	yes	no
competence	31	14	33	30	31	32
vision	26	16	29	25	29	23
collaboration	25	15	27	23	24	25
courage	15	13	10	17	17	13
humility	7	7	9	5	6	7
purpose	5	6	3	6	5	4
n=	1107	87	352	755	635	469

2. THE BOSSES WE WANT TO WORK FOR

In this era of increasing importance of good jobs, Christians were also asked what kind of boss they would like to work for. Respondents were given the same ten items to choose from. Interestingly, the same top two characteristics emerge as when asked to identify the most important leadership traits needed today: integrity (57%) and authenticity (47%).

But after that, the lists are different. Instead of the #3 to #5 factors being discipline, passion for God, and competence, Christians say they would want to work for a boss who is collaborative, competent, and humble. Passion for God drops from fourth place to seventh position, perhaps reflecting people's realization that the workplace is not necessarily filled with believers. Still, among evangelicals, finding a boss who is a believer remains the most important criterion in their job search.

Younger leaders are less likely than their older peers to look for bosses who have integrity or authenticity, but are slightly more interested in collaboration and purpose. They are much more likely than older adults to look for bosses who are humble.

What stood out among people who consider themselves to be leaders is that they are more interested than normal in serving for other leaders who live with integrity and lead with clear vision.

TABLE 2: CHARACTERISTICS OF A POTENTIAL BOSS

Question: Suppose you are offered a job from two different companies and you have to choose between two different kinds of bosses.

Remember, not everyone is perfect, but what are the 2 or 3 characteristics of the boss you would be most interested in working for? (Mark between 1 and 3 responses.)

	ALL CHRISTIANS	EVANGELICALS	AGE GROUP		SELF-DESCRIBED LEADER	
			18–39	40-plus	yes	no
integrity	57%	63%	51%	59%	59%	54%
authenticity	47	54	36	52	45	49
collaboration	39	15	41	37	36	42
competence	37	24	38	37	39	35
humility	26	27	32	23	23	30
vision	22	12	22	22	25	17
passion for God	22	68	20	22	22	20
discipline	22	15	25	21	24	20
courage	5	3	3	6	6	4
purpose	5	7	8	4	4	7
$n=$	1109	87	352	757	636	469

3. SELF-DESCRIBED LEADERS

Overall, more than half of Christians in this country say they are leaders (58%). About the same proportion of evangelicals (55%) believe they are leaders. There is no statistically significant difference based on the age of those interviewed.

The box below shows the demographic, theolographic, and psychographics of today's self-identified leaders.

It is somewhat striking that so few leaders think they have the kinds of leadership traits that are most needed today (i.e., integrity and authenticity). Or, to put it differently, they think of themselves as competent, disciplined collaborators, although those three traits are ranked as fifth, seventh, and third most important, respectively, in what is really needed today.

TABLE 3: SELF-DESCRIBED LEADER

Question: Do you personally consider yourself to be a leader?

	ALL CHRISTIANS	EVANGELICALS	AGE GROUP		SELF-DESCRIBED LEADER	
			18–39	40-plus	yes	no
yes	58%	55%	59%	57%	100%	0%
no	43	45	41	43	0	100
n=	1111	87	355	756	639	472

4. HOW LEADERS EVALUATE THEMSELVES

The survey asked those respondents who identified themselves as leaders to evaluate the *one* quality that best defines their leadership. The highest-ranked trait is competence (20%), followed by discipline (16%), collaboration (15%), integrity (15%), and authenticity (14%).

Appropriately, only 1 percent of Christians say they are best at being humble.

Evangelicals are cut from a different bolt of cloth, naming passion for God as far and away their best leadership quality (42%).

There are not any substantial differences by age group, with the only notable difference being that older leaders are actually slightly more likely than younger leaders to name authenticity (16% versus 11%, respectively).

TABLE 3A: PERSONAL LEADERSHIP QUALITIES

Question: Which *one* of the following leadership qualities best defines you?

| | ALL CHRISTIANS | EVANGELICALS | AGE GROUP | | SELF-DESCRIBED LEADER | |
			18–39	40-plus	yes	no
competence	20%	4%	19%	20%	20%	NA
discipline	16	8	20	15	16	NA
collaboration	15	11	13	16	15	NA
integrity	15	15	15	14	15	NA
authenticity	14	12	9	16	14	NA
passion for God	11	42	13	11	11	NA
vision	4	2	4	4	4	NA
purpose	3	2	5	2	3	NA
courage	2	*	1	2	2	NA
humility	1	4	2	1	1	NA
n=	*636*	*48*	*208*	*428*	*636*	*NA*

*indicates less than one-half of one percent

Leaders were also asked what they would most like to improve, using the same list of ten traits. The area where they want the most help is courage (27%), which is followed by a desire to grow in terms of discipline (17%), vision (15%), and passion for God (13%).

Evangelical leaders are most similar to the broader Christian market in this respect: they want to grow in terms of courage (27%), discipline (25%), passion for God (14%), and vision (9%). Younger leaders express a greater desire than older leaders to grow in terms of vision and purpose.

TABLE 3B: PERSONAL LEADERSHIP QUALITIES THAT NEED IMPROVEMENT

Question: Which *one* of the following qualities needs the most improvement in your own leadership?

| | ALL CHRISTIANS | EVANGELICALS | AGE GROUP | | SELF-DESCRIBED LEADER | |
			18–39	40-plus	yes	no
courage	27%	27%	25%	28%	27%	NA
discipline	17	25	17	17	17	NA
vision	15	9	20	12	15	NA
passion for God	13	14	10	14	13	NA
collaboration	9	4	10	9	9	NA
purpose	9	8	12	8	9	NA
humility	5	8	5	5	5	NA
competence	2	4	1	3	2	NA
integrity	2	2	1	3	2	NA
authenticity	1	0	1	1	1	NA
n=	*627*	*48*	*203*	*424*	*627*	*NA*

5. ATTITUDES ABOUT WORK, CALLING, AND LEADERSHIP

Finally, the research probed a number of different attitudes among Christians about work, calling, and leadership, set up as a series of agree/disagree statements.

Overall, 82 percent of Christians in America believe the nation is facing a crisis of leadership because there are not enough good leaders right now. Among evangelicals, 94 percent believe this to be true. Older Christians (84%) are most likely to assert this perspective, but the vast majority of younger Christians (78%) concur.

Most Christians (67%) believe the work they are doing is helping to create a better world; however, only one-fifth strongly agree. Evangelicals are even more sanguine about their efforts (82%) than the norm. The gap between younger (65%) and older Christians (68%) is statistically indistinct; yet, younger Christians are more likely than average to *strongly* concur with the statement (27%), perhaps reflecting the growing sensibility of "doing good" in the world.

When looking at the broad patterns, a sense of pride in their work was nearly a universal sentiment (98%). Nevertheless, when looking at the "agree strongly" response line, younger adults, evangelicals, and nonleaders could be criticized for showing some lower-than-average pride in their efforts.

The idea that their workplace has a clear vision that is easily understood by employees is an opinion strongly endorsed by only one-quarter of today's working Christians (23%). Evangelicals (35%) are slightly higher than normal, but the basic findings show that most people have only modest confidence or clarity about their company's vision.

Another survey question probed this opinion: the belief that God is calling them to do something else in terms of work, but they have not been willing to make a change yet because of their current life situation. Overall, 9 percent of working Christians agreed strongly and another 26 percent agreed somewhat, totaling one-third of today's employed Christians (35%) who are experiencing this kind of tension. Among younger Christians, nearly half (44%) are feeling this disconnect between the profession or job they would like and the realities of their current situation.

When asked if they believe that a person's calling lasts a lifetime, on balance, most people disagree rather than agree (68% versus 32%). In fact, only 4 percent strongly agree that one can see what a person is called to do from an early age. There are no notable differences by age, evangelical commitment, or leader status. Yet, instead of being an area where people have strongly formed opinions, it appears that most Christians just have not given this matter much thought. (Notice that most of the respondents choose the middle-ground answers of "somewhat," reflecting hedged bets.)

Choosing to interact regularly with an older mentor who gives great advice about work is even less common than having clear vision at work—only 16 percent of working Christians firmly assert they have this type of relational work-related guidance in place. Younger Christians are slightly more likely than older believers to have such mentorship in their lives (22% versus 12%), but there is still considerable room for growth. Interestingly, those who are leaders are twice as likely as nonleaders to say they have an older mentor in place to help navigate professional issues.

TABLE 5A: FEEL CALLED TO THEIR WORK

Question: Thinking about your current work, do you feel that you are "made for" or "called" to the work you currently do?

AMONG THOSE EMPLOYED	ALL CHRISTIANS	EVANGELICALS	AGE GROUP		SELF-DESCRIBED LEADER	
			18–39	40-plus	yes	no
feel "called" to my current work	34%	55%	31%	36%	38%	27%
do not feel called	19	18	27	14	18	21
not sure	13	16	16	12	13	15
never thought about it before	34	11	26	38	32	38
n=	593	47	216	377	383	211

Only about one-third of Christians (34%) feel called to the work they currently do (among those who are currently employed). This is much higher among evangelicals (55%), but still reflects a huge gap in terms of the Christian community's sense of divine purpose in their work.

Others say they "do not feel called" (19%), indicate they are "not sure" (13%), or admit they have "never thought about it before."

Younger Christians are less likely to feel called to their work than older Christians (31% versus 36%); however, interestingly, older Christians are even more likely than the younger set to confess they have never really even considered the idea of being called to their current role (26% versus 38%).

TABLE 5B: ATTITUDES ABOUT WORK, LEADERSHIP, AND CALLING

Question: Do you agree or disagree with the following statements:

ASKED AMONG ALL CHRISTIANS	ALL CHRISTIANS	EVANGELICALS	AGE GROUP		SELF-DESCRIBED LEADER	
			18–39	40-plus	yes	no
the nation is facing a crisis of leadership because there are not enough good leaders right now						
agree strongly	41%	73%	27%	48%	43%	37%
agree somewhat	41	21	51	36	38	45
disagree somewhat	15	4	20	12	14	15
disagree strongly	4	2	2	4	4	3
the work I am doing is helping to create a better world						
agree strongly	20	20	26	17	26	12
agree somewhat	47	62	39	51	49	44
disagree somewhat	24	8	30	22	19	32
disagree strongly	9	10	5	11	/	12
n**=	1116	87	358	758	639	472

TABLE 5C: ATTITUDES ABOUT WORK, LEADERSHIP, AND CALLING

Question: Do you agree or disagree with the following statements:

AMONG THOSE EMPLOYED	ALL CHRISTIANS	EVANGELICALS	AGE GROUP		SELF-DESCRIBED LEADER	
			18–39	40-plus	yes	no
I take personal pride in the quality of work that I do						
agree strongly	72%	65%	61%	77%	79%	58%
agree somewhat	26	26	34	21	19	39
disagree somewhat	1	0	2	*	1	1
disagree strongly	1	9	2	1	1	2
the place where I work has a clear vision that is easily understood by those working there						
agree strongly	23	35	27	21	22	24
agree somewhat	48	35	50	46	48	47
disagree somewhat	20	23	15	23	22	17
disagree strongly	9	7	9	10	8	12
I regularly interact with an older mentor who gives me great advice about work						
agree strongly	16	14	22	12	19	10
agree somewhat	33	37	38	30	31	35
disagree somewhat	31	22	25	35	31	31
disagree strongly	21	27	16	23	19	24

AMONG THOSE EMPLOYED	ALL CHRISTIANS	EVANGELICALS	AGE GROUP		SELF-DESCRIBED LEADER	
			18–39	40-plus	yes	no
I feel like God is calling me to do something else in terms of work, but I have not been willing to make a change yet because of my current situation in life						
agree strongly	9	8	12	8	9	10
agree somewhat	26	25	32	23	25	27
disagree somewhat	36	30	32	38	39	30
disagree strongly	29	37	25	31	27	33
n**=	595	47	216	377	383	211

*indicates less than one-half of one percent
**sample size varies with each question

NOTES

ESSENTIAL ONE | *CALLED*

1. Seth Godin. Catalyst Atlanta, 2010.

2. Christine Caine. Catalyst Podcast, Episode 143. www.catalystspace.com.

3. Erwin McManus. Catalyst Podcast, Episode 178. www.catalystspace.com.

ESSENTIAL TWO | *AUTHENTIC*

1. Reggie Joiner. Catalyst Podcast, Episode 189. www.catalystspace.com.

2. J.R. Vassar, Twitter post, August 3, 2012, 5:50 a.m., http://twitter.com/jrvassar.

3. Judah Smith. Catalyst Podcast, Episode 169. www.catalystspace.com.

4. Christine Caine. Catalyst Podcast, Episode 143. www.catalystspace.com.

ESSENTIAL THREE | *PASSIONATE*

1. Matt Chandler. Catalyst Podcast, Episode 182. www.catalystspace.com.

2. Louie Giglio. Catalyst Podcast, Episode 173. www.catalystspace.com.

3. John Piper, *Don't Waste Your Life* (Wheaton, IL: Crossway Books, 2003), 32.

ESSENTIAL FOUR | *CAPABLE*

1. Carmine Gallo, *The Innovation Secrets of Steve Jobs* (New York: McGraw-Hill, 2012), 199.

2. BrainyQuote®. © 2001-2012 BrainyQuote®. http://www.brainyquote.com/quotes/quotes/v/vincelomba385070.html.

3. My Incredible Website. http://myincrediblewebsite.com/the-quotable-walt-disney-do-what-you-do-so-well/.

ESSENTIAL FIVE | *COURAGEOUS*

1. Richard Stengel, "Mandela: His 8 Lessons of Leadership," *TIME*, July 9, 2008, http://www.time.com/time/magazine/article/0,9171,1821659,00.html.

2. James L. Snyder, *In Pursuit of God: The Life of A. W. Tozer* (Christian Publications, 1991), 14–15.

3. Daily Christian Quote. ©2012 I Lift My Eyes Web Ministries. http:// dailychristianquote.com/dcqcourage.html.

ESSENTIAL SIX | *PRINCIPLED*

1. Bob Goff, Twitter post, June 22, 2012, 8:19 a.m., http:twitter.com/bobgoff

2. Eugene Cho. Catalyst Dallas, 2011.

3. Louie Giglio. Catalyst Podcast, Episode 173. www.catalystspace.com.

4. Dave Ramsey, EntreLeadership (New York: Howard Books: 2011), 19.

5. John Maxwell. Catalyst Podcast, Episode 184. www.catalystspace.com.

ESSENTIAL SEVEN | *HOPEFUL*

1. BrainyQuote®. © 2001-2012 BrainyQuote®. http://www.brainyquote.com/ quotes/quotes/g/georgewash158551.html.

2. Priscilla Shirer. Catalyst Atlanta, 2011.

3. Cory Booker. "Hope Unhinged," *Linkedin*, October 11, 2012, http://www. linkedin.com/today/post/article/20121011182510-86654142-hope-unhinged

4. Simon Sinek, Twitter post, July 3, 2012, 10:52 a.m., http://twitter.com/ simonsinek.

ESSENTIAL EIGHT | *COLLABORATIVE*

1. Simon Sinek, Twitter post, July 5, 2012, 11:01 a.m., http://twitter.com/ simonsinek.

2. Goodreads. ©2012 Goodreads Inc. http://www.goodreads.com/ quotes/443803-the-next-best-thing-to-being-wise-oneself-is-to.

ABOUT THE AUTHOR

Brad Lomenick is lead visionary and president of Catalyst, one of America's largest movements of Christian leaders. Catalyst's mission is to equip, inspire, and release the next generation of leaders through events, resources, consulting, content, and connecting. In the last thirteen years, Catalyst has convened hundreds of thousands through high-energy and experiential leadership conferences across the United States.

Prior to running Catalyst, Brad spent five years involved in the growth of the nationally acclaimed *Life@Work* magazine and was a management consultant with Cornerstone Group where he worked with a variety of companies, organizations, and non-profit enterprises. Before that, he served as foreman for Lost Valley Ranch, a four-diamond working guest ranch in the mountains of Colorado.

Brad has had the privilege of interviewing dozens of the world's leading thinkers—including Malcolm Gladwell, Seth Godin, Rick Warren, and Dave Ramsey—through the Catalyst Podcast, which is free for download on iTunes or at catalystpodcast.com. He blogs about leadership, creativity, innovation, teamwork, personal growth, and more at bradlomenick.com.

Brad serves on the advisory boards for Suffered Enough, the A21 Campaign, Red Eye Inc., and Praxis. He holds a bachelor's degree from the University of Oklahoma and currently resides outside of Atlanta, Georgia.

You can follow him on Twitter at @bradlomenick and connect with Catalyst at catalystconference.com.

Consider bringing your team to a Catalyst event this year. With nine events spanning North America—three flagship Catalyst events and six Catalyst One-Days—there's something for everyone.

CATALYST

A CONVERGENCE OF NEXT GENERATION LEADERS

◇ CATALYST® PODCAST

The Catalyst Podcast delivers practical leadership and cultural insights through in-depth interviews with renowned leaders, sought-after speakers, and best-selling authors straight to you.

Conversations include:

ANDY STANLEY

CHRISTINE CAINE

EUGENE PETERSON

REV RUN

MARCUS BUCKINGHAM

TONY DUNGY

DAVID PLATT

JUDAH SMITH

PRISCILLA SHIRER

FRANCIS CHAN

SETH GODIN

CRAIG GROESCHEL

MATT CHANDLER

LOUIE GIGLIO

MALCOLM GLADWELL

FREE on iTunes. Subscribe Today.

Leadership Up Close
with Andy Stanley & Craig Groeschel

Creating A Healthy Culture DVD Set

We are irresistibly drawn to the remarkable: those cultures that shine because of their sense of purpose, the collective passion of their people, and the health of the organization. The Creating A Healthy Culture DVD set explores the intangibles that allow us to contribute to a culture which understands and lives its values, embraces change, nurtures authentic relationships, and fosters personal and organizational health. Each of the DVDs include a main talk, behind-the-scene interviews and discussion, and access to a participant's guide.

The Power of Momentum DVD Set

The Power of Momentum series takes a practical approach to unlocking the secrets of creating and sustaining momentum. Through examples and application, you will learn the systems and tactics that fuel personal, organizational, and ministry progress. Each of the four DVDs includes the main talk divided into four parts, as well as a going deeper session including behind-the-scenes interviews and discussion, and access to a participant's guide.

Groupzine Series

The Catalyst Groupzines are a collection of relevant articles, interviews, stories, features, and study guide segments around annual Catalyst event themes.

Volume VIII - The Making of a Leader

This study is for next generation leaders who understand the true calling of life and leadership to be a journey, not a destination. In order to lead well we must understand that our journey is a slow and steady climb, a long obedience in the same direction, and that *who* we are becoming is more important than *what* we are doing. Join us as we examine the qualities, events, and processes that make us the leader God has called us to be.

Voices DVD Series

Direct from the Catalyst stage, the Voices Series provides topic specific content to help individuals and teams grow in their leadership.

Dwell In Him
Matt Chandler

You Can Do This
Perry Noble

Systems, On Your Mark, & The Tension is Good
Andy Stanley